I0474575

Business

Management

Guidebook

Find the inner leader in you, become business guru

AMARPREET SINGH

Publisher - The Thought Flame

info@thethoughtflame.com

www.thethoughtflame.com

Table of Contents

Introduction

This book contains proven steps and strategies on how to become a leader in business management and how to understand the 7 Principles needed for successful leadership skills so that you can build a management team that you are proud of.

There are few things in this life more important than leadership in our short human lives. There are many reasons why leadership is important such as by having effective leadership helps to lead any nation when they are going through peril, it helps to make businesses grow and small run more efficiently, it enables corporations to fulfill their missions and it helps parents to raise their children to grow to be strong and smart adults.

When leadership is absent in every aspect of our lives, it can dramatically affect how our lives play out. In the absence of leadership, businesses run more slowly than they would normally, lose their way towards their mission, they lack necessary decision making processes that can affect the overall business, time management skills are lost and effective communication skills are lost.

Leaders in every aspect of our lives regardless if they are in our personal lives or if they are in our work lives can help to correct things that are not going well and can help to implement solutions to the problems we face on a daily basis. These leaders help to influence the behavior of the people around them, help to alter the outcomes of upcoming events that are happening and help to overcome any resistance a company or household may meet.

In all honesty all of us recognize the importance of leadership in one way or another regardless of it is our own political leaders, leadership in our office setting or in our own home. We recognize the need for having excellent leadership skills as a whole and for some, we strive to become that leader and have complete control over our surrounding.

Regardless of where you are, having exceptional leadership skills in every aspect of your life is more important than you may realize. In this eBook we will discuss the importance of leadership in business management, the 7 different principles needed for leadership skills and how exceptional leadership skills can help you to motivate others so that you can build a team that everybody wants to be a part of.

Thanks again for downloading this book, I hope you enjoy it!

Chapter 1: The Importance of Leadership

So the question remains: what exactly does leadership mean? Leadership is the process in which one person is chosen to help influence the attitude, behavior and thoughts of the people around them. People, who are leaders help to guide us in the right direction, help to inspire us to work harder and they help us to see what lies ahead of us. It is no secret that without leadership every human on the planet would quickly disintegrate into conflict and argument. This is because every human being sees the world differently and thus act differently in their own actions, behaviors, feelings and our own different solutions.

Leadership helps to unite humans as a whole and help to point every single one of us in the same direction to work towards a common goal. However, a leader is not a leader without a certain amount of followers and these followers will not come immediately to stand behind a person right off the bat. For example take Winston Churchill who lived during the 1930's. When he first came into light he urged his fellow Englishmen that Hitler was an imminent threat and he was a person that needed to be dealt with immediately. Many people around him believed that Hitler was a man that could be reasoned with and that would not have them start a war with Germany. However, they were wrong. These people believed that the future with Hitler around was not a dangerous one and was one that could be lived in peace. As a result of this these people despised Winston Churchill for forcing them to believe that they needed to engage in a world and face danger in order to face Hitler.

During that time Churchill had very few followers and many rejected his leadership.

However, sooner than they would have liked Hitler and Germany went too far in their attacks and war became inevitable. It was only then that Winston was acclaimed for his incredible foresight into the future and eventually became the prime minister of the United Kingdom during World War II. It was only then that nearly every Englishmen accepted his leadership and followed him willingly.

When it comes to identifying true leadership, it is often hard due to many instances of false leadership. All that false leadership is that it is a form of pretending and the person "leading" has no problem dropping their duty the moment they face trouble. Winston Churchill was the example of great and real life leaders. However, there are many people in this world who wish to become leaders, but they aren't meant for that kind of destiny. These false leaders claim that they are leaders and they pretend they are setting a set course of direction and inspiring the people that follow them. More often than not however, are pretending.

There is an old saying that claims, "if you want to become a leader, find a parade and run to the front." This saying can be used to describe a false leader as even though you run to the front of a parade, you are actually not leading it. Even in a parade a person is not really leading it unless they are choosing the direction it is going towards. A false leader may be at the front of a wave of people, but unless they are leading a direction to which the people are following, they are not leading them.

When it comes to leadership, many people do not realize that it can be used for both good and ill will. An example of this is Hitler himself as he was able to lead the German people that followed him but he led them in an evil direction. Hitler was a great leader, but he used his leadership skills for terrible uses and was responsible for murdering and torturing innocent people.

In the business world, leadership skills that are used for bad purposes are used to exploit others. In charitable organizations these people use their leadership skills to help benefit themselves rather than the people they claim they are trying to help. Either way there are different ways leadership skills can be used, but it is important to understand that they can be used to bring good things to people around the actual cause as well as evil things such as war and famine.

Why Is Leadership Important?

Leadership is important for a variety of different reasons. Regardless of where the leadership is needed whether it is at home or in a work environment leadership is important in every aspect of our everyday lives. Some of the reasons why it is important include:

1. Helps to provide a direction for both our families and our co-workers to follow when we face unstable times in our lives.

2. Help to set a positive example of what honesty is truly about and what it means to have it in everyday life.

3. Helps us to provide a safe and stable balance in our everyday lives between our work and family.

4. Leaders help to provide a stable and safe environment to help children to learn and grow up to be productive and intelligent adults.

5. Help the people in your life to start their own business, find whatever their passion may be or help the people around you to lose weight in order to become the people they wish to became as they grow older.

6. Help everyone around you to follow both their passions and their dreams.

In today's world people need to realize that in order to seize the numerous and valuable opportunities around them, those who are destined to need to rise to lead others in order to achieve greatness for themselves. Though we may believe that only certain men and women who possess the qualities needed to lead people around them, ordinary people can become leaders as well, as long as they put their minds to it. Ordinary people are the ones who have the power to create great changes that the world needs, solve problems that others cannot solve and lead those that need their help. The only way ordinary people can do this however is to believe in themselves and work to helping the people around them to work towards a better future.

Chapter 2: The Seven Essential Principles of Leadership

In order to have effective leadership skills, there are seven essential principles that every leader must follow. As with anything else, leadership is not something that can just be done without thinking about it first. While leadership may come naturally for some people, for others who are thrust into a leadership position must practice and use these principles if they wish to succeed in leading others toward a brighter and more efficient future.

1. Must Be Patient

In order to become a great leader, a person must have great patience and must have excellent self-control when handling difficult situations. The act of leading others is not an act that can use a "soft" touch, as that will not help others to follow you towards the direction you want to lead them to. As a leader, even if you lead with love you must remember to hold the people around you accountable for their actions, but you must remember to do it with both respect and patience. Remember, when you lead others to follow you, you do not do it simply because of the performance you want, you do it to protect the dignity of the people who follow you.

If you are in a work setting, then your primary goal should be to train your employees to the best of your ability, whether it is in public or in private and it should be done with respect, patience and love. If you are leading your family at home then the same must be done as these people know you intimately and it could have catastrophic results if you lead them wrong.

2. Must Be Kind

In order to lead people, you must lead them with kindness and attempt to show encouragement and enthusiasm not matter what you are trying to accomplish. By leading with kindness you are creating and maintaining the right atmosphere in your environment whether you are at work or at home, so that your family or employees are able to deliver whatever it is you want them to deliver such as paperwork, behavior or customer service.

The best way I can describe this is to say for example a person you are leading is a bank account. Your primary goal is to make a deposit into their emotional "account" so that that account can grow into something you never would have imagined. When you show kindness to those around you, the goal is to give at least three praises to everyone admonishment. Using this ratio helps to ensure that you are showing the right amount of kindness to those around you. Kindness eventually leads to the people around you becoming loyal and enthusiastic to your cause and will help them to follow you willingly.

3. Must Be Trusting

Another thing that you need to do in order to become a great leader is to gain the trust of those you wish to lead and to place confidence in them that you are an ideal leader. Trust works in two ways. In order for a business or a home to run efficiently, a leader must trust the people around them and the same goes for the people looking to the person who is leading them.

In order to gain other people's trust and to give them the confidence needed to follow you the key is to listen well to each and every person and to do so with interrupting their thoughts with your own ideas. Another thing to keep in mind is to also let the people around you to make their own decisions in the acts they are primarily responsible for as this will help them to be confident in your own leadership skills.

By trusting the people around you and by them trusting your leadership skills helps to build a positive environment and will eventually lead to positive morale and trust in the long run.

4. Must Be Unselfish

Another thing to keep in mind in order to become a great leader is to be unselfish and to think less of yourself. You need to think of the people around you more often than yourself from time to time. The same goes for the organizations around you as well. When it comes to leadership, it means that those of us who wish to lead are given the responsibility of giving up our time and our resources responsibly and properly. This responsibility often includes the responsibility of delegating which nearly every leader will need to participate in. Not only will delegating be rewarding and efficient for you, but it will also help you to become selfless and help others to view you as such. This helps to show others the respect you have towards them and make them much more willingly to follow you in the long run.

One way you can think of those around you other than yourself is to start and organization within your own organization in which you help the people around you who are in need. You can donate to these people and help countless people around you when they really need it.

5. Must Be Truthful

In order to become the best leader that you can be the key thing to do is to be as truthful as possible and make sure you know how to act in a corporate setting and in your own personal setting. This is often referred to as leading with love as you lead other by giving them truthful and loving feedback in order to make whatever they are doing better for both only the organization, but for themselves as well.

For many people who are not used to leading will love will feel that this is strange and foreign for them and greatly puts them out of their own comfort zone.

However, it is perhaps one of the healthiest ways to lead and helps to give leaders an opportunity to grow their organization or home life to great lengths. When leading the people around you, leading with honesty and giving them truthful feedback about their performance regardless of what they will feel is a way to show the people that you care about them and want to lead them in the right direction with love.

6. Don't Forget To Forgive

When it comes to having excellent leadership skills, leaders must not forget to be forgiving and to forget about holding on to grudges, as this is something that has the potential to harm your leadership over others. While forgiving people is sometimes an agonizing process and hardly ever leads to a happy ending, it is something that needs to be done regardless. I am not at all telling you that you need to ignore whatever rules and policies you have set forth. What I am suggesting is that you try to soften your own heart just a little bit and be willing to forgive others regardless of the circumstance.

While it may be the easiest thing to do in the world, forgiving people is the right thing to do in the long run.

7. Be Dedicated

One of the most important things you can do as a leader is to make sure that you stay dedicated to the task at hand and to make sure that you stick to your values regardless of the circumstance. If you are the type of leader who leads the people that follow you with love and others do not understand what it is you are doing, simply forget them and continue leading them your way. Leading the people that follow you in a dedicated fashion is very important regardless if you are given approval or not because others are most likely to follow you willingly than others that do not lead in your fashion. Remember, a wise leader is one that dedicates himself or herself to the task at hand regardless of what other people think and choose to lead their people with love. Leading with dedication is one of the best ways to lead any organization and while it may not be easy, it is the right thing to do.

Chapter 3: The Importance of Motivation

What is motivation? Motivation is an internal process that a person can make that will help them reach their certain goal. Motivation itself is not something that can be observed directly by other people, but instead is more like a mental act. In fact motivation itself can be noted by how a person acts and feels towards a certain situation.

There have been many instances when researchers have tried to study the way motivation acts on the human mind and tried to explain what motivation actually does to a person and more often than not they fail at coming up with a logical explanation. Some of the theories that researchers have used include Maslow's Hierarchy and drive reduction theories.

In this chapter we will discuss these different theories and you will learn for yourself what each theory is and how it leads to the understanding of motivation itself.

Drive Reduction Theories

When it comes to drive reduction theories in terms of motivation these theories suggest that people act only to reduce their needs and to maintain a healthy physiological state. To better understand this just take eating for example. People need to eat in order to reduce the amount of food they will need to eat during the entire day. Homeostasis itself is what drive the drive reduction theories. So what is Homeostasis? Homeostasis is the maintenance of the body itself and helps to maintain physiological equilibrium.

While drive reduction theories help us to understand what it can do for people, it does fail to explain several important factors of motivation itself. Some of these factors include:

1. People are not always motivated by their own internal needs

What this means is that people have no problem doing things for certain causes than they do for others. So for example many people out there will go on a hunger strike for a cause whether it is to save an historical monument or for their own rights and these people will do this despite them feeling starved. These people will harm their own bodies for the cause or belief they have.

2. People continue to feel motivated even though their internal needs have been met

When it comes to motivation, it is such a fickle thing. It doesn't make sense to many people and this is one factor that continues to baffle researchers to this day. What this factor means is that a person can continue doing things even if they don't need it. For example take a person who has just eaten. If they are bored or simply if they want it, they can continue eating without even feeling hungry.

3. People can be motivated by both external and internal incentives

When it comes to becoming motivated, humans have a knack to motivate themselves to get exactly what they want. For example say a man or a woman wishes to lose weight in order to live a healthier life. They can easily motivate themselves to eat a healthy salad rather than an unhealthy cheeseburger, that way they can work easily towards their weight loss goals. People can do this with pretty much anything such as smoking, exercise or even their own career.

Intrinsic vs. Extrinsic Motivation

When it comes to motivation itself, it can either be intrinsic, extrinsic or even both. The difference between these two types of motivation defines both greatly. Intrinsic motivation is when motivation is used for the sake of acting out alone. The best way to understand this is to take a group of poetry writers for example. These people do not write poetry because they have to, rather because they simply enjoy it.

On the other hand, extrinsic motivation is when motivation is used to receive great rewards. As an example take a writer who has written many books for a certain amount of years. The end goal for this writer is to either become published, make lots of money or to become famous off of their writing.

Regardless of what kind of motivation is used to help a person thrive in every aspect of their life, each kind of motivation needs a variety of incentives in order to prove successful. What is an incentive? An incentive is a stimulus from the environment that helps people to act in a particular way towards their own goal. For example an incentive could be getting an A on an exam so that a person can pass their class for the semester.

Chapter 4: Leadership and Motivation In Business Management

So far we have learn that both leadership and motivation play a critical role in how people act and how they in turn produce high quality work regardless if they are at home or at work. We know that motivation is defined as a factor that helps not only to motivate people, but also helps in maintaining and control another person's overall behavior. Motivation itself is used, as a way to get something a certain person wants such as financial freedom, money in a savings account or the best presentation ever seen.

Leadership is likewise as important as motivation as a leader is responsible for motivating the people that follow them. So how does motivation and leadership help people in a workplace setting? In this chapter you will learn for yourself how important motivation is in a workplace setting and how you can help motivate the people that you work with.

Motivation in The Workplace

Motivation is a stimulus that is used in the workplace to help energize and control the behavior of the employees working there. Using proper motivation can help to control what kind of outcome an employer is looking for whether it is an increase in sales or an increase in work output. From a professional standpoint motivation itself is a big deal as what the employees do on an everyday basis presents the overall future of the company or organization.

While it is no secret that motivation is important in every workplace, it is often difficult to explain its effectiveness in an empirical sense. While knowing that an increase in motivation equals to high productivity output, it is hard to pinpoint exactly how much motivation one should use and no one can measure a person's own personal drive to accomplish something. However, it has been commonly accepted by nearly every company and organization around in the world that the more motivated employees are, the more they will achieve in a single work week.

That is why it is extremely important to understand the management of motivation itself so that any organization and company can succeed in their business in the long run as it helps to maximize the overall effectiveness of its common human resources.

Salary is perhaps one of the most commonly used motivating factors out there today as employees will work for pretty much any organization or company as long as the pay is good. However, pay alone does not guarantee that a person will work to the greatest of their potential. According to Herzberg's theory it claims that while salary is enough to keep employees at the same corporation for many years, it may not be enough to motivate employees to work to the best of their overall ability.

Employees who are only motivated by only salary and benefits are more likely to slack off in their work overtime. This helps employers to understand exactly how and what motivates their employees so that they can create a successful team or business for the long run. This is where an employee's internal and external motivations come into play and can help employers to understand what it is that helps their employees to produce more high quality work.

Internal and External Motivation Factors

There are many benefits that properly motivated employees will bring to any company that they work for. Some of these benefits include:

1. Employees will find new and creative ways to improve the overall quality of their work.

2. Employees that are constantly motivated always pay close attention to every detail on a project, regardless of the project's overall size.

3. Employees that are constantly motivated tend to be more productive and efficient with the work they produce.

In conclusion motivating the employees that work for you will not only help you to retain a higher level of innovation, but it will also help your employees to produce a higher quality of work and will have a higher level of efficiency. I know that these different kinds of benefits may seem broad and a bit vague, but it helps to prove the point that motivating the employees that work for you does not have a down side. There is no cost whatsoever to motivate employees nor does it take much effort to do as long as you have the right managers in place that have excellent leadership and motivational skills.

Five Ways To Motivate Your Employees

To put it simply, there are plenty of unmotivated employees working their butts off out there in the workforce. A recent national study that was recently conducted showed that less that 1 in 4 employees working felt unengaged from their work, which of course showed there, was ample room for high quality improvement. The study also found that management, who are the primary individuals responsible for ensuring that their employees work to the best of their ability, were the ones responsible for having low motivation levels in their area of expertise.

In this section we will discuss five different ways you can motivate your employees as well as five different ways to de-motivate them.

1. Try To Align Employees Individual Economic Interests with The Company's Overall Performance

While this isn't as easy to accomplish as the other motivational ways we will discuss, but it is nonetheless one of the most important. A leader will be able to align their employee's individual economic interests with their company's performance as long as they have the right mindset and determination to do it.

One of the best ways to do this is to try to enact an incentive compensation program that will enable all employees regardless of their position, to benefit from the program. This is a great way to boost motivation in your company and a great way to create a working team environment.

2. Try To Be Interested In The Path That Each Of Your Employees Want To Take On Their Career

When an employee has a manager that seems to truly care about their future and cares exactly where their career is headed, you will be surprised how much of an impact it can make to that employee. The best way to show your employees that you care about their future is to mentor your employees, coach them and offer additional training. Employees will value this kind of help and will feel motivated to work harder every single day.

3. Try To Be Interested In Your Employees Work and Life Balance Act

One of the best things managers can do is attempt to be somewhat flexible in the way they make weekly schedules. To do this try to keep in mind and try to be understanding of your employees commitments to their own family, important doctor's appointments, etc. By showing that you take these important commitments into consideration will go a long way in earning you the respect of your employees.

4. Try To Simply Listen

Now listening may seem like a simple thing to do and it can be as long as you do it properly. Truly listen to your employees regardless what they are talking to you about. Listen as they voice their own opinions on how to improve job performance, other employee problems, their own frustrations or concerns, and any conflicts they may be having with other employees.

The most difficult thing you will have to do here is to separate the junk from the important matters that need to be addressed, such as the things that pertain to your workplace. While listening can wear you out sometimes, remember that is is all apart of the job and you just need to grit your teeth and get through it as best as you can.

5. Follow the Golden Rule

The golden rule states to do unto others as you would have done unto you. This easily applies to the workforce and the way that you treat you subordinates is very important as they are the ones responsible for doing the job that you need done in order to make the company run smoothly. By following the golden rule it will show that you have respect for your employees and in turn they will have respect for you.

<u>Conclusion</u>

Thank you again for downloading this book!

The importance of motivation and leadership in both the workplace and at home is one of the most important things any person can do to benefit the lives of the people around them. It is what makes our live run smoothly on a day-to-day basis and what helps us to reach the goals we have set for ourselves to improve our future.

Leadership in itself is what many of strive to do both at home and in the workplace, but let's face it. Everybody is not cut out to be a leader. Leadership involves an exact science and steps that need to be followed in order to do it correctly as how you act will impact how the people who follow you will view you.

Without motivation itself you cannot expect to become a great leader. Motivation is the thing that helps to drive the people around you to act in the way you want. There are different things you can do to motivate the people around you such as following the Golden Rule, respecting others, giving them compliments and reassuring them daily and understanding the commitments that they may have. However, while you can motivate these people, you can also de-motivate them, which is something that should try to be avoided at all costs.

Regardless of how you motivate or demotivate the people around you, it is extremely important to keep in mind that becoming a leader and motivating the people around you is hard work, but nevertheless it is extremely important.

Hopefully by reading this eBook you learned how you can become and effective leader and what you can do to motivate the people around you, so that you and the people following you are given the chance to reach your future goals in the years to come.

Finally, please take the time to share your thoughts by posting a review on Amazon. It would be greatly appreciated!

Thank you and good luck!

About Us

The Thought Flame is committed to add value to its customers through various books, online courses and other resources. You can learn more about us and our books at www.thethoughtflame.com.

Don't forget to check out our amazing **online video courses** at www.thethoughtflame.com/courses/ to take your knowledge to another level.

To check out our **extraordinary collection of diet/cookbooks**, visit http://www.thethoughtflame.com/category/non-fictional/cookbooks/ .

As a part of our valued relationship with our customers, we keep providing you free promotional books, courses and other stuff on subscribing with us on our site. We have a strict anti-spam policy and assure you no spam mails will be sent to your mailbox.

To subscribe with us, visit www.thethoughtflame.com.

Like our work and would like to say thanks?

Buy us a cup of coffee at www.thethoughtflame.com/coffee/

Author

Amarpreet Singh is an avid learner and his passion for education has made him travel, work and study all across the world. He holds three masters degrees, including MBA, from top universities in Asia.

He is author of dozens of books, many of which are Amazon's bestseller, varying in various topics and categories. He also teaches many online courses having thousands of students across the world.

He has a keen interest in international affairs, economics, global poverty and politics, financial markets and entrepreneurship, and strives to be part of a community that shares the same passion.

He has worked as consultant with organizations like Airbus and The World Bank.

He loves travelling and learning about new cultures, and has been fortunate to live/work/travel/study in countries like India, China, Korea, US, South Africa, Japan, Philippines, Singapore, Canada etc., and learn about the culture and lifestyle in each of them.

To check out more of his work, visit

www.thethoughtflame.com

www.ingramcontent.com/pod-product-compliance
Lightning Source LLC
Chambersburg PA
CBHW021445170526
45164CB00001B/404